Thank you for reading our South Korean Heritage Songbook. We created the Heritage Songbook Series to promote musical understanding between children, parents, and educators around the world.

We hope you spend many happy hours with the children in your care singing these songs and listening to the accompanying recordings at fiddlefoxmusic.com. There, you'll also find coloring pages and other printable activities for all the books in our Heritage Songbook Series.

We've also included color-coded sheet music so young instrumentalists can play and sing along. We recommend using colored rainbow bells that match up with our notation system, but you can also use colored stickers on piano keys or ukulele frets if you would like.

Happy Music-Making!

From the Fiddlefox

www.fiddlefoxmusic.com

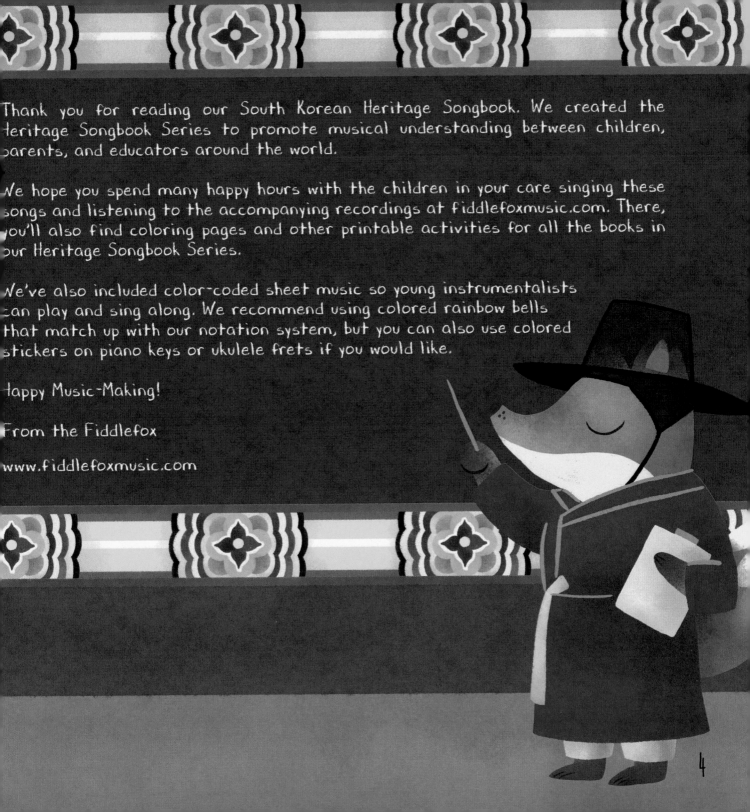

4

TABLE OF CONTENTS

SOUTH KOREAN
HERITAGE SONGBOOK

Fiddlefox

한국에 온 것을 환영해
HANGUK-E ON GEOT-EUL HWANYEONG-HAE
WELCOME TO KOREA!

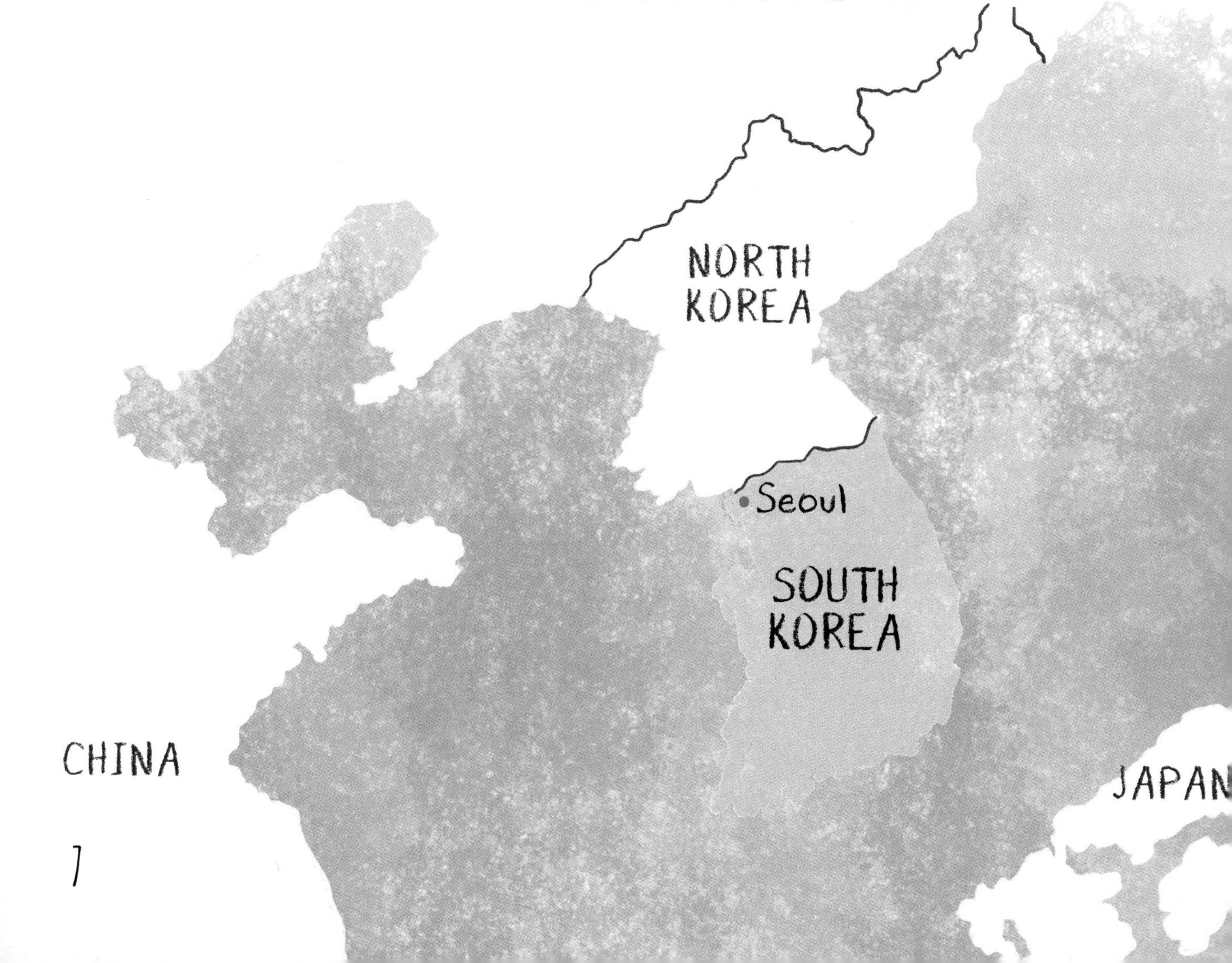

NORTH
KOREA

• Seoul

SOUTH
KOREA

CHINA

JAPAN

7

Korea is a peninsular country surrounded by China to the north, the Yellow Sea to the west, and the Sea of Japan on the east. People have lived in Korea for 10,000 years, likely coming down from Siberia and China. Korea is a small country, but it is very crowded. There is not much room for wild animals there today, but you can still find cranes, musk deer, and if you're very lucky, a rare endangered amur leopard.

Korea is a nation of treasured traditions and new, exciting technology and popular culture. Korean pop music (K-Pop for short) is listened to all over the world.

In 1950, a great war caused Korea to be split into two countries: North Korea and South Korea. Though the countries are still divided, we like so many, hope that they will unite in peace someday.

8

산토끼
SAN TO KKI
HILL BUNNY

산토끼 토끼야
San to kki, to kki ya
Hill bunny, did you hide

어디를 가느냐
Eo di leul ga neu nya
Down in the snow so white?

깡충깡충 뛰면서
KKANG CHUNG KKANG CHUNG TTWI MYEON SEO
Found you, found you, in the snow!

어디를 가느냐
Eo di leul ga neu nya
Wait, now where did you go?

NOTES USED
C D E F G C

SAN TO KKI
HILL BUNNY

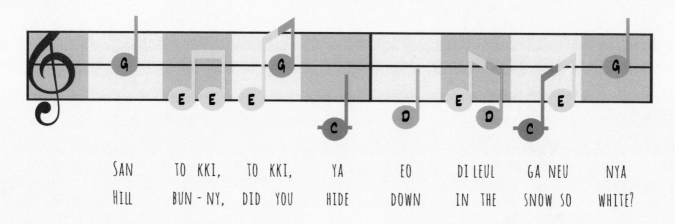

| San | to kki, | to kki, | ya | eo | di leul | ga neu | nya |
| Hill | bun - ny, | did you | hide | down | in the | snow so | white? |

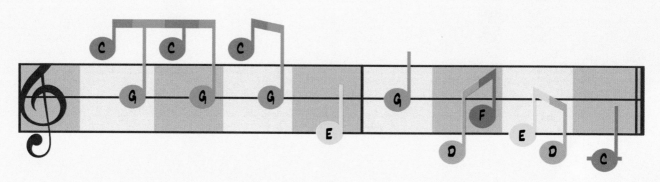

| Kkang chung, | kkang chung, | ttwi myeon | seo | eo | di leul | ga neu | nya |
| Found you, | found you, | in the | snow! | Wait, | now where | did you | go? |

13

아리랑
ARIRANG

아리랑, 아리랑,
아라리요
ARIRANG, ARIRANG,
ARARIYO . . .

15

아리랑 고개로 넘어간다
ARIRANG GOGAERO NEOMUHGANDA
OVER THE ARIRANG MOUNTAIN YOU GO

나를 버리고 가시는 님은

Nareul beorigo gasineun nimeun

Oh, my love you have gone on your way

ARIRANG

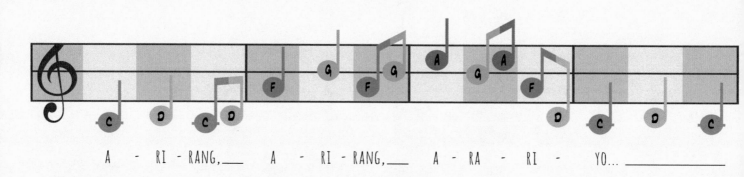

A - RI - RANG,___ A - RI - RANG,___ A - RA - RI - YO... _____

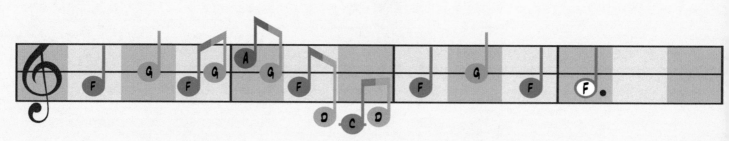

A - RI - RANG,___ GO - GAE - RO___ NEO - MUH - GAN - DA.
O - VER THE __ A - RI - RANG,___ MOUN - TAIN - YOU - GO.

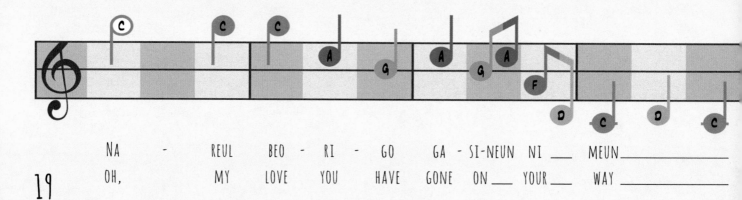

NA - REUL BEO - RI - GO GA - SI-NEUN NI ___ MEUN_____
OH, MY LOVE YOU HAVE GONE ON___ YOUR___ WAY _____

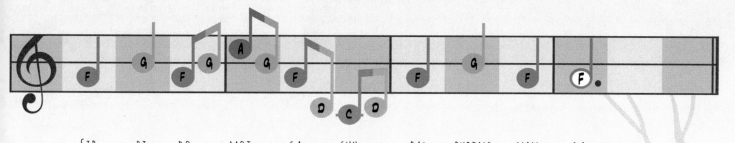

SIB - RI - DO ___ MOT - GA - SUH___ BAL - BYEONG - NAN - DA.
THOUGH YOU ROAM, ___ WE WILL - BE TO - GE - THER SOME DAY.

20

달 따러 가자
DAL TTA LUH GA JA
TIME TO CATCH THE MOON

얘들아 나오너라 달 따러 가자
YE DEUL A NA O NUH LA DAL TTA LUH GA JA
EVERYONE! EVERYONE! TIME TO CATCH THE MOON!

장대 들고 망태 메고 뒷동산으로
JANG DAE DEUL GO MANG TAE ME GO DWIT DONG DAN EUH RO
PUT IT IN A BURLAP SACK, I KNOW WE'LL TAKE IT SOON.

뒷동산에 올라가 무등을 타고
DWIT DONG SAN E OL LA GA MU DEUNG EUL TA GO
REACH IT WITH A BAMBOO STICK HIGH ABOVE THE HILLS

23

장대로 달을 따서 망태에 담자
JANG DAE LO DAL EUL TTA SEO MANG TAE E DAM JA
THEN WE CAN LIGHT OUR HOUSE WITHOUT A HEFTY BILL

Dal Tta Luh Ga Ja
Time to Catch the Moon

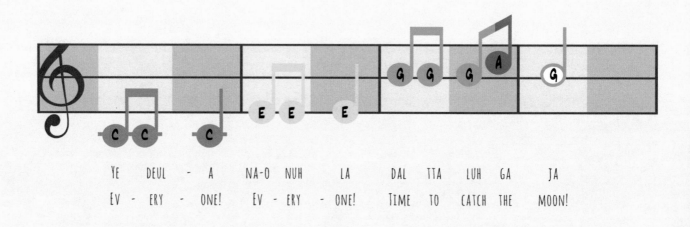

YE	DEUL	-	A	NA-O	NUH	LA	DAL	TTA	LUH	GA	JA
EV	- ERY	-	ONE!	EV	- ERY	- ONE!	TIME	TO	CATCH	THE	MOON!

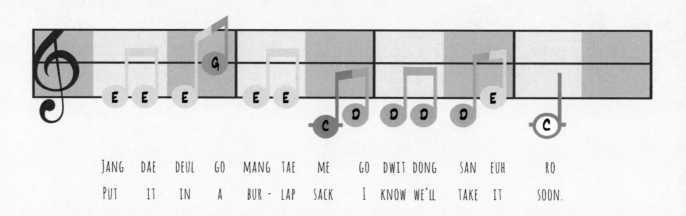

JANG	DAE	DEUL	GO	MANG	TAE	ME	GO	DWIT	DONG	SAN	EUH	RO
PUT	IT	IN	A	BUR	- LAP	SACK	I	KNOW	WE'LL	TAKE	IT	SOON.

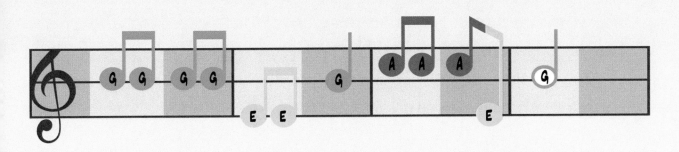

Dwit DONG SAN E OL LA GA DEUNG EUL TA GO
Reach it WITH A BAM - BOO STICK HIGH A - BOVE THE HILLS

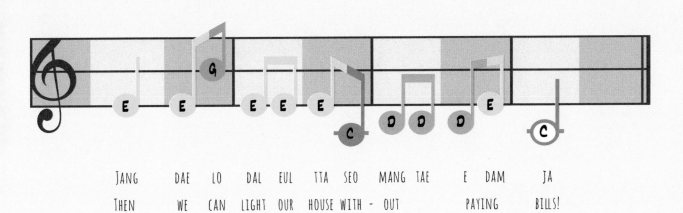

Jang DAE LO DAL EUL TTA SEO MANG TAE E DAM JA
Then WE CAN LIGHT OUR HOUSE WITH - OUT PAYING BILLS!

26

봄나들이
BOM NA DEUL I
SPRINGTIME SONG

나리 나리 개나리
NA LI NA LI GAE NA LI
GOLDEN FLOWER, NEWBORN LEAF

27

입에 따다 물고요
IB E TTA DA MUL GO YO
HOPPING WITH IT IN YOUR BEAK

28

병아리떼 종종종
BYEONG A LI TTE JJONG JJONG JJONG
LITTLE CHICKIES! RUN! RUN! RUN!

봄나들이 갑니다
BOM NA DEUL I GAB NI DA
SPRINGTIME CAN BE SO MUCH FUN!

BOM NA DEUL I
SPRINGTIME SONG

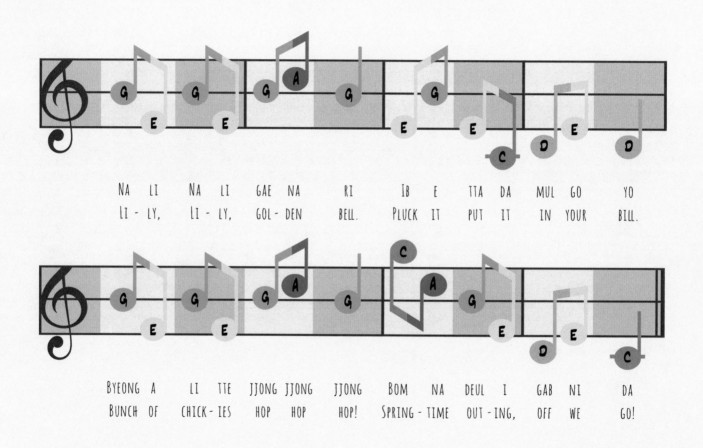

BRING A WORLD OF MUSIC HOME WITH
FIDDLEFOX WORLD HERITAGE SONGBOOKS!

Available on iBooks, Kindle and Spotify!
www.fiddlefoxmusic.com